# Healing the Heart:

## Overcoming Emotional Trauma Through Faith in God

Dr. Latina C. Campbell

Print ISBN: 978-1-955312-80-6

eBook ISBN: 978-1-955312-81-3

Printed in the United States of America

Story Corner Publishing & Consulting, Inc.

Chesapeake, VA 23321

Storycornerpublishing@yahoo.com

www.StoryCornerPublishing.com

# Dedication

I dedicate this book to my oldest daughter, Caliyah. I love you to the moon and back!

"Love is patient, love is kind. It does not envy, it does not boast, it is not proud. It does not dishonor others, it is not self-seeking, it is not easily angered, it keeps no record of wrongs. Love does not delight in evil but rejoices with the truth. It always protects, always trusts, always hopes, always perseveres. Love never fails. But where there are prophecies, they will cease; where there are tongues, they will be stilled; where there is knowledge, it will pass away."

1 Corinthians 13:4-8 NIV

# Table of Contents

# Introduction

## Healing the Heart

Life has a way of leaving its marks on us. Sometimes, those marks go deeper than the surface—they reach into the very core of our being, creating wounds that no one else can see. Emotional trauma can feel like an invisible prison, holding us captive to pain, fear, and despair. It might stem from betrayal, loss, abuse, or moments when the world seemed to shatter around us. Whatever the source, the weight of trauma can be suffocating.

But the truth is this: you are not alone. God sees your pain. He understands the depth of your hurt, and He wants to walk with you through the journey of healing. The Bible tells us in Psalm 34:18, "The Lord is close to the brokenhearted and saves those who are crushed in spirit." His nearness is not a distant promise but a present reality for those who seek Him.

This book is an invitation—a call to lay your burdens at the feet of Jesus and let His love transform your heart. It is not about denying the pain you've endured or pretending everything is okay. Rather, it's about confronting your brokenness with the confidence that God's grace is greater than your suffering.

## The Journey of Healing

Healing from emotional trauma is not an easy road, nor is it a quick fix. It requires courage, honesty, and trust in the One who created you. The good news is that God specializes in making all things new. Through His Word, His presence, and His promises, He offers a pathway to restoration and peace.

In this book, we will explore practical steps to invite God into the healing process. You will learn how to:

1. **Acknowledge the pain**: Naming your trauma is the first step toward healing.

2. **Surrender to God**: Trust Him with your broken pieces and allow Him to mend what has been shattered.

3. **Find strength in scripture and prayer**: Discover the promises of God that bring hope and renewal.

4. **Forgive and release**: Let go of bitterness and embrace the freedom of forgiveness.

5. **Walk in wholeness**: Step into the abundant life God has planned for you.

This journey will be both spiritual and practical, combining faith-based guidance with actionable steps. Along the way, we'll draw on examples from the Bible, showing how God faithfully healed and restored those who trusted Him. From David's psalms of anguish to Jesus' compassion for the broken, the scriptures are filled with testimonies of God's power to heal the heart.

## God's Promise for You

No matter how deep the hurt, no matter how impossible healing might seem, God's love is deeper and stronger. He has a plan for your life—a plan for hope, joy, and peace. Jeremiah

29:11 reminds us, "For I know the plans I have for you, declares the Lord, plans to prosper you and not to harm you, plans to give you a future and a hope."

This is not just a promise for someone else. It is a promise for you. If you are ready to take the first step toward freedom and healing, this book will be your guide. Together, we will invite God into the darkest corners of your pain and allow His light to bring renewal.

Let's begin this journey of healing, knowing that with God, nothing is impossible. The road ahead may be challenging, but with every step, you will grow stronger, find deeper peace, and discover the boundless love of the One who calls you His own.

Are you ready to embrace the healing God has for you? Let's begin.

# Chapter 1:

# Understanding Emotional Trauma

Emotional trauma is more than just a fleeting sadness or a passing moment of distress—it is a profound wound that impacts your mind, body, and spirit. It stems from experiences that overwhelm your ability to cope, leaving you feeling powerless, broken, and trapped. Trauma can take many forms, whether from a single devastating event or prolonged exposure to hardship, neglect, or abuse.

For many, trauma feels like an isolating experience, something no one else could possibly understand. But the truth is, even in the Bible, we find people who faced unimaginable pain, yet God walked with them, bringing healing and restoration. By looking at their lives, we can begin to understand the nature of emotional trauma and the hope that God offers.

## The Nature of Emotional Trauma

Trauma affects us on multiple levels:

1. **Mentally**: It can distort our thinking, leaving us stuck in cycles of fear, anxiety, or self-doubt. You might replay the event over and over in your mind or feel constantly on edge, as though the trauma is happening all over again.

2. **Physically**: Trauma often manifests in the body through fatigue, sleeplessness, or chronic pain. It can feel like your body is carrying the weight of your past experiences.

3.  **Spiritually**: Trauma can shake your faith, making you question God's goodness or wonder if He's truly with you. It can feel like a wall has been built between you and Him.

Recognizing how trauma affects these areas is the first step in understanding the depth of your pain and God's desire to heal you completely.

## Biblical Examples of Trauma and Hope

The Bible doesn't shy away from the reality of suffering. Instead, it offers us examples of individuals who faced trauma but found restoration in God:

1.  **Job**: Job's life was marked by unimaginable loss—his children, his wealth, and even his health. He wrestled with deep despair and questioned God, yet ultimately, he experienced God's faithfulness and healing. Job's story reminds us that it's okay to grieve and question, but we must also trust that God is working even when we don't understand.

2.  **David**: Known as a man after God's own heart, David faced betrayal, loss, and fear for his life. His psalms often express raw, unfiltered emotions: "My tears have been my food day and night" (Psalm 42:3). But David consistently brought his pain to God, finding comfort and hope in His presence.

3.  **Joseph**: Betrayed by his own brothers, sold into slavery, and unjustly imprisoned, Joseph endured years of suffering. Yet, he remained faithful to God, and in the end, he was able to see how God used his pain for a greater purpose: "You

intended to harm me, but God intended it for good"
(Genesis 50:20).

These stories remind us that no matter how dark or overwhelming our circumstances may seem, God is always present, working behind the scenes to bring about healing and redemption.

## The Promise of God's Healing

God's desire is not for you to remain trapped in the pain of your trauma. He promises healing and restoration to all who seek Him. Psalm 147:3 says, "He heals the brokenhearted and binds up their wounds." This isn't just a poetic sentiment—it's a reality you can experience when you invite God into your brokenness.

Healing doesn't always happen instantly. Sometimes, it's a process, requiring patience and perseverance. But God is faithful, and His power to heal knows no bounds. He is not only able to mend your heart but to make it stronger and more resilient than before.

## Practical Reflection: Identifying the Source of Your Trauma

Before you can heal, it's important to understand the root of your pain. Spend time reflecting on the following questions:

1. What specific events or experiences have caused emotional wounds in your life?

2.  How has this trauma impacted your thoughts, behaviors, and faith?

3.  Where do you see evidence of God's hand in your journey, even in the midst of your pain?

This process of self-awareness, paired with prayer, opens the door for God to begin His healing work in you.

## Key Takeaway: God Meets You Where You Are

No matter how deep the pain or how long you've carried it, God is not afraid of your brokenness. He is the Great Physician, the One who can take what feels shattered and turn it into something beautiful. As we move forward in this book, know that understanding your trauma is not the end of the story—it is the beginning of God's redemptive work in your life.

Let this truth anchor you: *God sees you, He knows your pain, and He is ready to heal you.* All you need to do is take the first step and trust Him with your heart.

# Chapter 2:

# Acknowledging the Pain

Healing from emotional trauma begins with an essential yet often difficult step: acknowledging your pain. Many people attempt to bury their hurt, suppress their emotions, or pretend everything is fine. But true healing cannot occur until we face the reality of our suffering. In this chapter, we'll explore why it's crucial to name and confront your trauma, how the Bible models this process, and practical steps to begin this transformative journey.

## Why Acknowledging Pain is Necessary

### 1. Suppressed Pain Festers

When we ignore or deny our pain, it doesn't simply disappear—it finds ways to manifest in our lives, often in unhealthy ways. Suppressed trauma can lead to emotional outbursts, physical ailments, and spiritual numbness. Acknowledging your pain brings it into the light, where God can begin to heal it.

### 2. Acknowledgment is the Door to Healing

Naming your pain is not a sign of weakness; it is an act of courage and faith. By admitting that you are hurting, you are opening the door for God to step in and begin His work of restoration. Psalm 34:18 reminds us, "The Lord is close to the brokenhearted and saves those who are crushed in spirit." But we must first admit that we are brokenhearted for Him to come close.

### 3. God Meets Us in Our Honesty

Throughout scripture, God honors raw and honest expressions of pain. He does not expect us to hide our emotions or put on a brave face. When we pour out our hearts to Him, He listens with compassion and moves toward us with healing.

## Biblical Examples of Acknowledging Pain

### 1. David's Psalms of Lament

David, a man after God's own heart, often cried out to God in anguish. In Psalm 13, he asked:
*"How long, Lord? Will you forget me forever?*
*How long will you hide your face from me?"*
David didn't shy away from his pain—he named it, expressed it, and brought it before God. His honesty led to healing and deeper intimacy with the Lord.

### 2. Hannah's Tears

Hannah, barren and ridiculed, wept bitterly before the Lord. In 1 Samuel 1:10, it says, "In her deep anguish Hannah prayed to the Lord, weeping bitterly." Her willingness to confront and express her pain opened the way for God to respond with compassion, eventually blessing her with a son, Samuel.

### 3. Jesus at Gethsemane

Even Jesus, in the Garden of Gethsemane, acknowledged His overwhelming sorrow: "My soul is overwhelmed with sorrow to the point of death" (Matthew 26:38). He didn't hide His anguish but brought it to the Father, showing us that it's okay to be vulnerable in God's presence.

## Practical Steps to Acknowledge Your Pain

1. **Create a Safe Space for Reflection**

Set aside intentional time to reflect on your pain. Find a quiet place where you can be alone with your thoughts and God. Ask Him to reveal areas of hurt you may have suppressed or forgotten.

2. **Name Your Trauma**

Write down the events or experiences that have caused you pain. Be specific. Naming your trauma helps to bring clarity and allows you to see patterns that may have shaped your life.

3. **Express Your Emotions Honestly**

Whether through journaling, speaking with a trusted friend, or praying aloud, give yourself permission to feel and express your emotions. Remember, God can handle your anger, grief, and questions.

4. **Invite God Into Your Pain**

Pray for God to meet you in your brokenness. Tell Him exactly how you feel and ask for His healing presence. A simple prayer might be:

*"Lord, I am hurting. I feel broken and overwhelmed by my pain. Please meet me here and help me to heal. I surrender this hurt to You and trust in Your love and faithfulness."*

# Obstacles to Acknowledging Pain

### 1. Fear of Vulnerability

Many people fear that confronting their pain will make them feel weak or out of control. But vulnerability is not a weakness; it is a strength that allows God to work in your life.

### 2. Shame or Guilt

Shame often tells us that we're at fault for our pain or that we don't deserve healing. But Romans 8:1 reminds us, "There is now no condemnation for those who are in Christ Jesus." You are not defined by your trauma; you are defined by God's love for you.

### 3. Numbing Through Distractions

In our modern world, it's easy to avoid confronting pain by staying busy or numbing ourselves with entertainment, substances, or other distractions. But true healing requires intentional stillness and reflection.

## A Biblical Practice: Lamenting

Lamenting is a Biblical way of processing pain. It involves:

1. **Crying Out**: Be honest about your pain and present it to God.

2. **Bringing Your Complaint**: Tell God exactly what you are struggling with, just as David did in the Psalms.

3. **Choosing to Trust**: End your lament by reaffirming your faith in God's goodness and sovereignty.

For example:

*"Lord, I feel abandoned and hurt. Why has this happened to me? But I know You are faithful, and I trust You will bring me through this storm."*

## Key Takeaway: Pain is a Place Where God Meets You

Acknowledging your pain is not an act of defeat—it is an act of faith. It's saying, "God, I trust You enough to bring my brokenness to You." When you face your hurt with honesty and invite God into those raw places, you create room for Him to work miracles in your heart.

The journey of healing begins here, with this simple but profound step: recognizing that you are hurting and trusting that God's love is big enough to heal even the deepest wounds.

Take heart—your pain does not have the final word. God does, and His word declares that He is close to the brokenhearted, ready to bind up your wounds and lead you into freedom.

# Chapter 3:

# The Power of Surrender

Healing from emotional trauma requires not just acknowledgment of pain but also the willingness to let go and surrender it to God. Surrendering is not about ignoring your trauma or pretending it didn't happen; rather, it is about entrusting your pain to the One who has the power to redeem it. Surrender is an act of faith and a crucial step toward healing because it shifts the burden from your shoulders to God's.

In this chapter, we will explore what it means to surrender your pain, why it's essential for healing, and how to practically and spiritually release your trauma into God's hands.

## What Does Surrender Mean?

Surrendering your pain means giving God full access to your brokenness and trusting Him to heal it. It involves:

1. **Letting Go of Control**: Acknowledging that you cannot heal yourself and that you need God's intervention.

2. **Releasing Bitterness and Anger**: Choosing to forgive others and yourself, freeing your heart from the weight of resentment.

3. **Trusting God's Plan**: Believing that God can bring purpose out of your pain and trusting His timing for your healing.

Surrender is not passive resignation—it's an active decision to place your trauma, fears, and uncertainties in God's capable hands.

## Why Surrender is Essential for Healing

### 1. We Weren't Meant to Carry the Burden Alone

Jesus said, "Come to me, all you who are weary and burdened, and I will give you rest" (Matthew 11:28). Emotional trauma is a heavy burden, but God never intended for you to carry it alone. Surrendering allows you to rest in His strength instead of relying on your own.

### 2. Surrender Brings Freedom

Holding onto pain, resentment, or control can keep you trapped in the past. By surrendering, you release these chains and step into the freedom that Christ offers. Galatians 5:1 says, "It is for freedom that Christ has set us free."

### 3. Surrender Invites God's Healing Power

When you surrender your trauma, you create space for God to work. As long as you hold tightly to your pain, you may unintentionally block His healing. By letting go, you invite His transformative power into your heart.

## Biblical Examples of Surrender

### 1. Jesus in the Garden of Gethsemane

In one of His most vulnerable moments, Jesus modeled surrender when He prayed, "Father, if you are willing, take this cup from me; yet not my will, but yours be done" (Luke 22:42).

Even in anguish, Jesus trusted the Father's plan, showing us the power of surrender in the face of suffering.

### 2.  **Paul's Thorn in the Flesh**

Paul, who faced countless hardships, surrendered his pain to God, saying, "My grace is sufficient for you, for my power is made perfect in weakness" (2 Corinthians 12:9). Instead of resisting his struggles, Paul found strength in surrendering them to God.

### 3.  **Job's Faithful Surrender**

Job, after losing everything, declared, "The Lord gave and the Lord has taken away; may the name of the Lord be praised" (Job 1:21). His willingness to surrender his pain and trust God led to his eventual restoration.

## Practical Steps to Surrender Your Pain

### 1.  **Admit Your Need for God's Help**

Begin by acknowledging that you cannot heal yourself. Pray honestly:
*"Lord, I cannot carry this pain on my own. I need You to take this burden from me and heal my heart."*

### 2.  **Release Your Resentment**

Holding onto anger or bitterness keeps you tied to the source of your pain. Surrendering means forgiving those who have hurt you—not for their sake, but for yours. Ask God to help you forgive, even when it feels impossible.

3. **Surrender Daily**

Surrender is not a one-time event but a daily practice. Each day, make the conscious choice to place your trauma in God's hands. Say, *"Lord, today I give You my pain, my fears, and my doubts. I trust You to guide me toward healing."*

4. **Replace Control with Trust**

Letting go of control can be scary, but trust is the foundation of surrender. Reflect on Proverbs 3:5-6:
*"Trust in the Lord with all your heart and lean not on your own understanding; in all your ways submit to him, and he will make your paths straight."*

5. **Engage in Worship and Prayer**

Worship is a powerful way to surrender your heart to God. Through songs and prayer, you can release your pain and be reminded of God's goodness and faithfulness.

## Obstacles to Surrender

1. **Fear of Vulnerability**

It can be frightening to let go of pain, especially if it has become part of your identity. You might wonder who you'll be without it, but God wants to redefine you as whole, healed, and loved.

2. **Desire for Control**

Trauma often leaves us feeling powerless, and holding onto control can feel like self-protection. But true healing comes when we release control to the One who is sovereign.

### 3. Doubt in God's Timing

Surrendering doesn't mean healing will happen overnight. Trusting God's timing can be challenging, but His ways are higher than ours (Isaiah 55:8-9).

## A Prayer of Surrender

Use this prayer as a guide to help you release your pain to God:

*Heavenly Father, I come before You with a heavy heart. The pain I carry feels overwhelming, and I don't know how to heal on my own. Today, I choose to surrender my trauma to You. I release my anger, my fear, and my need for control. I forgive those who have hurt me, and I forgive myself for holding onto this pain for so long. I trust You, Lord, to take my brokenness and create something beautiful. Give me the strength to surrender daily and the faith to believe in Your healing power. In Jesus' name, amen.*

## Key Takeaway: God Works in Surrender

Surrender is not the end of the story—it is the beginning of God's work in your life. When you lay your burdens at His feet, you make room for His healing, peace, and restoration. Trust that He will carry you through this process and bring you to a place of wholeness.

Remember, surrender is not about losing—it's about gaining freedom, healing, and a closer relationship with God. As you release your pain into His hands, you will discover the profound truth that His grace is sufficient and His power is made perfect in your weakness.

# Chapter 4:

# Forgiving Yourself and Others

Forgiveness is one of the most challenging yet transformative aspects of healing from emotional trauma. Trauma often leaves a trail of anger, resentment, guilt, and shame—emotions that can trap you in the past and hinder your ability to move forward. Forgiveness is not about excusing the harm done to you or forgetting the pain; rather, it is about releasing yourself from the chains of bitterness and allowing God to restore your peace.

This chapter will delve into what forgiveness is, why it is essential for healing, and how to approach the process of forgiving both others and yourself.

## What Forgiveness Is—and What It Is Not

1. **What Forgiveness Is**

   - Forgiveness is a choice to release resentment and the desire for revenge.

   - It is an act of obedience to God, trusting Him to handle justice in His perfect way and timing.

   - Forgiveness is a step toward freedom, allowing you to live unburdened by the weight of anger or guilt.

2. **What Forgiveness Is Not**

   - Forgiveness is not condoning or excusing the harm done to you.

- It does not mean you must forget the trauma or reconcile with someone who is unsafe.

- Forgiveness is not a one-time act; it may require ongoing commitment as emotions resurface.

## Why Forgiveness Is Essential

### 1. Forgiveness Sets You Free

Holding onto bitterness or anger is like drinking poison and expecting the other person to suffer. When you forgive, you release the emotional and spiritual burden, freeing yourself to heal.

### 2. Forgiveness Aligns You with God's Will

The Bible commands us to forgive because we have been forgiven. Ephesians 4:32 says, *"Be kind and compassionate to one another, forgiving each other, just as in Christ God forgave you."* Forgiveness is a reflection of God's love and grace in your life.

### 3. Forgiveness Restores Your Peace

Unforgiveness keeps you tied to the person or event that hurt you. Forgiving allows you to let go of that connection, restoring your peace and redirecting your focus toward God's healing power.

## Biblical Examples of Forgiveness

### 1. Jesus on the Cross

Even in His suffering, Jesus exemplified forgiveness when He prayed, "Father, forgive them, for they do not know what they are doing" (Luke 23:34). His example shows us that forgiveness is not about the worthiness of the offender but about obedience to God and the freedom it brings.

## 2. Joseph Forgiving His Brothers

Joseph, betrayed by his brothers and sold into slavery, had every reason to harbor resentment. Yet, when he faced them years later, he said, "You intended to harm me, but God intended it for good" (Genesis 50:20). His forgiveness allowed him to move forward and see God's purpose in his pain.

## 3. The Parable of the Unforgiving Servant

In Matthew 18:21-35, Jesus tells a parable emphasizing the importance of forgiving others as we have been forgiven by God. The story reminds us that forgiveness is a reflection of the grace we've received.

# Forgiving Others

## 1. Acknowledge the Pain

Before you can forgive, you must recognize and validate the hurt you've experienced. Minimizing the pain or pretending it didn't happen can hinder genuine forgiveness.

## 2. Choose Forgiveness

Forgiveness is not about how you feel—it is a decision. Ask God for the strength to forgive, even when it feels impossible.

## 3. Pray for the Person Who Hurt You

Praying for those who have wronged you is a powerful act of obedience and humility. It shifts your focus from their offense to God's ability to work in both their life and yours.

4. **Set Healthy Boundaries**

Forgiveness does not mean allowing someone to continue to harm you. Establishing boundaries is a necessary part of protecting your heart and fostering healing.

## Forgiving Yourself

1. **Recognize God's Grace**

Many people struggle to forgive themselves, burdened by guilt or regret. But if God, in His infinite love, has forgiven you, who are you to withhold forgiveness from yourself? Romans 8:1 assures us, *"There is now no condemnation for those who are in Christ Jesus."*

2. **Confess and Surrender Your Guilt**

If your guilt stems from sin or mistakes, confess them to God and ask for His forgiveness. 1 John 1:9 promises, *"If we confess our sins, he is faithful and just and will forgive us our sins and purify us from all unrighteousness."*

3. **Renew Your Mind**

Replace thoughts of shame with the truth of God's Word. Meditate on scriptures that affirm your identity in Christ, such as 2 Corinthians 5:17: *"Therefore, if anyone is in Christ, the new creation has come: The old has gone, the new is here!"*

4. **Extend Grace to Yourself**

Healing is a process, and you will make mistakes along the way. Treat yourself with the same compassion and grace that God extends to you.

# Practical Steps Toward Forgiveness

### 1. Write It Down

Make a list of the people or situations you need to forgive, including yourself. Write down what happened, how it made you feel, and why you're choosing to forgive.

### 2. Pray for Strength

Ask God to help you forgive, acknowledging that forgiveness is a supernatural act that often requires His intervention.

### 3. Release the Burden

Visualize yourself handing your pain, anger, or guilt to God. Say aloud, *"Lord, I release this burden to You. I choose to forgive and trust You with my healing."*

### 4. Repeat as Needed

Forgiveness is a journey, not a one-time event. When painful memories resurface, reaffirm your decision to forgive and release the burden to God again.

## Obstacles to Forgiveness

### 1. Unresolved Pain

Forgiving doesn't mean ignoring the need to process your trauma. Work through your emotions with God and, if necessary, with a trusted counselor or support system.

### 2. Desire for Justice

It's natural to want justice for the wrongs done to you, but vengeance belongs to the Lord. Romans 12:19 reminds us, *"Do* not take revenge, my dear friends, but leave room for God's wrath."

3. **Fear of Vulnerability**

Forgiveness can feel like letting your guard down, but remember, you're entrusting your pain to God, who is your ultimate protector.

## A Prayer for Forgiveness

Use this prayer to guide you in forgiving yourself and others:

*Heavenly Father, I come to You with a heavy heart. The pain I've carried from my trauma feels overwhelming, but I trust that You are greater than my hurt. Today, I choose to forgive [name or situation]. I release the anger, bitterness, and resentment I've been holding onto, and I place it in Your hands. Help me to forgive myself as well, remembering that I am covered by Your grace. Give me the strength to forgive, even when it feels difficult, and remind me of Your love and mercy. In Jesus' name, amen.*

## Key Takeaway: Forgiveness Leads to Freedom

Forgiveness is not about letting someone "off the hook"; it's about freeing yourself from the chains of bitterness and guilt. When you forgive, you reflect the heart of God, who has forgiven you completely and unconditionally.

As you forgive others and yourself, you will experience the peace and healing that only God can provide. Remember, forgiveness is a journey, and God walks with you every step of the way, leading you toward wholeness and freedom.

# Chapter 5:

# Embracing God's Love as a Foundation for Healing

At the heart of every healing journey is the profound and life-changing truth of God's love. His love is not just a concept or a feeling; it is an unshakable, transformative reality that meets you in your brokenness and brings restoration. Emotional trauma often leaves you feeling unworthy, abandoned, or unlovable, but God's love speaks directly to those wounds, affirming your value and offering a new identity as His beloved child.

In this chapter, we will explore the nature of God's love, its role in your healing process, and practical ways to embrace and experience it in your daily life.

## The Nature of God's Love

### 1. God's Love is Unconditional

Unlike human love, which is often conditional or based on performance, God's love is constant and unchanging. Romans 5:8 says, *"But God demonstrates his own love for us in this: While we were still sinners, Christ died for us."* This means that God loves you fully, even in your brokenness.

### 2. God's Love is Healing

Psalm 147:3 reminds us, *"He heals the brokenhearted and binds up their wounds."* God's love goes beyond comfort; it actively restores and redeems the parts of you that have been hurt by trauma.

### 3. God's Love is Personal

God knows you intimately and loves you individually. Isaiah 43:1 declares, *"Do not fear, for I have redeemed you; I have summoned you by name; you are mine."* His love is not distant or abstract—it is deeply personal and specific to you.

### 4. God's Love is Everlasting

Nothing can separate you from God's love. Romans 8:38-39 assures us, *"For I am convinced that neither death nor life, neither angels nor demons, neither the present nor the future, nor any powers... will be able to separate us from the love of God that is in Christ Jesus our Lord."* This everlasting love is a firm foundation for your healing.

## Why God's Love is Essential for Healing

### 1. God's Love Rebuilds Your Identity

Trauma can distort how you see yourself, often leaving you feeling worthless or broken. God's love reminds you of your true identity: a cherished and valuable child of God. 1 Peter 2:9 affirms, *"You are a chosen people, a royal priesthood, a holy nation, God's special possession."*

### 2. God's Love Replaces Fear with Security

Trauma often produces fear and anxiety. God's perfect love drives out fear and provides a sense of safety and security. 1 John 4:18 says, *"There is no fear in love. But perfect love drives out fear."*

### 3. God's Love Restores Hope

Emotional trauma can make it hard to believe in a better future. God's love renews your hope, reminding you that He has a plan to prosper you and give you a future filled with peace (Jeremiah 29:11).

### 4. God's Love Empowers Forgiveness

As discussed in the previous chapter, forgiveness is a vital step in healing. Embracing God's love enables you to forgive yourself and others because you are filled with His grace and compassion.

## Biblical Examples of God's Healing Love

### 1. The Prodigal Son

In Luke 15:11-32, the prodigal son returns home after making terrible mistakes, expecting rejection. Instead, his father welcomes him with open arms and unconditional love. This story illustrates God's readiness to embrace you, no matter how far you feel from Him or how broken you may be.

### 2. The Woman at the Well

In John 4, Jesus meets a Samaritan woman who feels rejected and ashamed due to her past. He speaks to her with love and truth, offering her living water that satisfies her deepest thirst. His love transforms her, and she becomes a bold witness to others.

### 3. The Healing of the Bleeding Woman

In Luke 8:43-48, a woman who has suffered for years reaches out to touch Jesus in faith. His love and power heal her completely. This story demonstrates that no matter how long you've been hurting, God's love can bring healing and restoration.

## How to Embrace God's Love in Your Healing Journey

### 1. Spend Time in God's Word

The Bible is filled with reminders of God's love for you. Meditate on scriptures like Psalm 136:26, *"Give thanks to the God of heaven. His love endures forever."* Let His Word reshape your understanding of His love and your identity.

### 2. Pray for a Deeper Revelation of His Love

Ask God to help you experience His love in a personal way. Pray, *"Lord, open my heart to fully receive Your love. Help me to see myself through Your eyes and to trust in Your unwavering affection for me."*

### 3. Surround Yourself with Community

Being part of a faith-based community allows you to experience God's love through the encouragement, prayers, and support of others. Hebrews 10:24-25 urges us to build one another up in love.

### 4. Reject Lies and Embrace Truth

Trauma can cause you to believe lies about yourself or God. Replace these lies with the truth of God's Word. When you feel unworthy, remind yourself of Zephaniah 3:17: *"The Lord your God is with you, the Mighty Warrior who saves. He will take great delight in you; in his love he will no longer rebuke you, but will rejoice over you with singing."*

5. **Express Gratitude**

Practicing gratitude for God's love can help you internalize it. Keep a journal of ways you've experienced His love in your life, whether through answered prayers, acts of kindness, or moments of peace.

6. **Worship Him**

Worship allows you to connect with God's love on a deeper level. Through music, prayer, and praise, you can express your love for Him and feel His love in return.

## A Prayer to Embrace God's Love

*Father God, I thank You for Your unfailing love. When I feel unworthy or broken, remind me of Your promises and the truth of who I am in You. Help me to experience Your love in a personal and tangible way. Heal the places in my heart that feel distant or guarded, and fill them with Your peace. Teach me to trust in Your love as the foundation of my healing. Thank You for loving me completely and unconditionally. In Jesus' name, amen.*

## Obstacles to Embracing God's Love

1. **Feelings of Unworthiness**

Trauma can make you feel undeserving of love. Remember, God's love is not based on your worthiness but on His character.

2. **Difficulty Trusting God**

Past experiences of betrayal or abandonment may make it hard to trust in God's love. Be patient with yourself and ask God to help you grow in trust over time.

3.  **Believing Lies About God**

Trauma may cause you to question God's goodness or believe He is distant. Combat these lies with the truth of His Word and seek His presence in prayer.

## Key Takeaway: God's Love is the Anchor of Your Healing

No matter how deep your wounds or how long you've carried them, God's love is greater. His love provides the foundation for your healing, reminding you that you are seen, known, and cherished.

As you embrace His love, you will find strength to release your pain, courage to trust Him with your future, and peace to rest in His care. Let His love be the constant in your healing journey, guiding you toward wholeness and joy.

# Chapter 6:

# Finding Hope in God's Word

The Bible is a living, breathing testament to God's love, promises, and faithfulness. In the midst of emotional trauma, when hope seems distant or unattainable, God's Word becomes a lifeline. This chapter explores how the Scriptures can anchor you in truth, uplift your spirit, and reignite your hope in God's plan for your life.

## God's Word as a Source of Hope

### 1. Hope Rooted in God's Promises

The Bible is filled with promises that remind us of God's unchanging character and His faithfulness to His people. One of the most powerful assurances is found in Jeremiah 29:11, *"For I know the plans I have for you," declares the Lord, "plans to prosper you and not to harm you, plans to give you hope and a future."*

When trauma leaves you feeling hopeless, God's Word reminds you that He has a good plan for your life. His promises are not conditional on your circumstances—they are anchored in His love for you. Clinging to these promises gives you the strength to face each day, knowing that brighter days are ahead.

### 2. A Light in the Darkness

Psalm 119:105 says, *"Your word is a lamp to my feet and a light to my path."* In times of emotional trauma, when darkness seems to overshadow every aspect of life, Scripture illuminates the way forward. God's Word provides clarity, direction, and a sense of peace that transcends understanding.

Each time you open the Bible, you allow God to speak directly into your heart, replacing fear and confusion with His truth and guidance.

## Scriptures That Restore Hope

The Bible offers countless verses that speak directly to the wounded heart. Here are a few passages to meditate on when hope feels distant:

1. **Psalm 34:18**: *"The Lord is close to the brokenhearted and saves those who are crushed in spirit."*

This verse is a reminder that God is near to you in your pain. You are not alone; His presence surrounds you even in your darkest moments.

2. **Romans 8:28**: *"And we know that in all things God works for the good of those who love him, who have been called according to his purpose."*

Even in the midst of suffering, God is at work. He is weaving the threads of your pain into a greater story of redemption and purpose.

3. **Isaiah 40:31**: *"But those who hope in the Lord will renew their strength. They will soar on wings like eagles; they will run and not grow weary, they will walk and not be faint."*

Hope in God renews your strength. It lifts you above your circumstances and gives you the endurance to press forward.

4. **Lamentations 3:22-23**: *"Because of the Lord's great love we are not consumed, for his compassions never fail. They are new every morning; great is your faithfulness."*

Each new day is a reminder of God's unfailing love and mercy. No matter what yesterday held, today is an opportunity to experience His grace afresh.

# Engaging with Scripture for Healing

### 1. Meditation and Reflection

Meditating on God's Word allows it to sink deeply into your heart and mind. Choose a verse or passage that speaks to your situation, and spend time reflecting on its meaning. Ask yourself:

- What is God saying to me through this verse?

- How can I apply this truth to my life right now?

Let the words of Scripture wash over you, replacing lies with truth and despair with hope.

### 2. Praying Scripture

One of the most effective ways to engage with God's Word is through prayer. Turn the verses you read into personal prayers, inviting God to work in your heart. For example:

- *"Lord, Your Word says You are close to the brokenhearted. Be near to me in my pain and remind me of Your presence."*

- *"Father, I trust that You are working all things for my good, even when I don't understand. Help me to see Your purpose in my life."*

### 3. Journaling God's Promises

Write down the verses that resonate with you and revisit them regularly. Journaling allows you to document God's promises and reflect on how His Word speaks to your unique journey. Over time, you'll see how these truths have sustained you and brought you hope.

## Jesus/ Yeshua: The Living Word of Hope

The ultimate source of hope in the Bible is Jesus Christ Himself. John 1:1 tells us, *"In the beginning was the Word, and the Word was with God, and the Word was God."* Jesus/ Yeshua is the Living Word, and His life, death, and resurrection are the foundation of our hope.

Through Christ, we have the assurance that no matter how deep our pain, God's love is greater. Jesus carried the weight of our sin and suffering so that we could experience freedom and restoration. His victory over death is proof that hope is never lost.

When you feel overwhelmed by trauma, remember the invitation Jesus/ Yeshua extends in Matthew 11:28-30: *"Come to me, all you who are weary and burdened, and I will give you rest. Take my yoke upon you and learn from me, for I am gentle and humble in heart, and you will find rest for your souls."*

## Practical Steps to Build Hope Through God's Word

### 1. Create a Daily Bible Routine

Consistency is key to finding hope in God's Word. Set aside time each day to read, meditate, and pray. Even a few minutes spent in Scripture can have a profound impact on your outlook.

2. **Memorize Key Verses**

Hiding God's Word in your heart (Psalm 119:11) equips you to combat discouragement and despair. Memorize verses that speak to hope and recall them whenever you face moments of doubt or fear.

3. **Join a Bible Study or Small Group**

Community provides accountability and encouragement. Studying the Bible with others allows you to gain new insights and share your journey with people who can support and pray for you.

4. **Declare God's Word Aloud**

Speak Scripture over your life. Declaring God's promises out loud reinforces His truth and helps you stand firm against the lies of the enemy.

## Hope That Endures

Hope rooted in God's Word is unshakable because it is based on His unchanging character and eternal promises. Psalm 130:5 says, *"I wait for the Lord, my whole being waits, and in his word I put my hope."*

No matter how broken or weary you feel, God's Word reminds you that hope is alive. It renews your faith, strengthens your heart, and points you to the ultimate source of healing and restoration: Jesus Christ.

Let the Scriptures guide you, comfort you, and fill you with the unending hope that comes from knowing and trusting God.

Through His Word, He is speaking life, healing, and peace into your soul. Will you open your heart to receive it?

# Chapter 7:

# Renewing Your Mind Through God's Word

The battle to overcome emotional trauma often takes place in the mind. Trauma can leave a lasting imprint on your thoughts, shaping how you see yourself, others, and even God. Negative thought patterns, lies, and fears often replay like a broken record, holding you captive to the pain of the past. However, God offers you the power to renew your mind through His Word.

Renewing your mind is not about ignoring reality or pretending that everything is fine. It is about replacing the lies and distortions caused by trauma with the truth of who God is, who you are in Him, and the promises He has made. In this chapter, we'll explore why renewing your mind is essential, how God's Word transforms your thoughts, and practical ways to cultivate a renewed mindset.

## Why Renewing Your Mind is Essential for Healing

### 1. The Mind is the Gateway to Transformation

Romans 12:2 teaches, *"Do not conform to the pattern of this world, but be transformed by the renewing of your mind."* Healing requires a shift in how you think. Renewing your mind aligns your thoughts with God's truth, enabling you to walk in freedom and peace.

2. **Trauma Alters Your Thought Patterns**

Trauma often reinforces negative beliefs, such as "I am not good enough," "I am unlovable," or "The world is unsafe." These thoughts can become strongholds that affect your emotions and actions. Renewing your mind breaks these strongholds and replaces them with God's truth.

3. **Your Thoughts Shape Your Reality**

Proverbs 23:7 says, *"For as he thinks in his heart, so is he."* What you dwell on in your mind influences how you see yourself, your relationships, and your future. Renewing your mind helps you see yourself and your circumstances through God's perspective.

## How God's Word Transforms Your Thoughts

1. **The Word is Truth**

Jesus said in John 17:17, *"Sanctify them by the truth; your word is truth."* God's Word provides a reliable foundation for replacing the lies of trauma with unchanging truth.

2. **The Word Brings Freedom**

John 8:32 promises, *"Then you will know the truth, and the truth will set you free."* When you meditate on God's Word, it breaks the chains of fear, shame, and doubt, setting you free from the mental prison of trauma.

3. **The Word Renews Your Hope**

Psalm 119:114 declares, *"You are my refuge and my shield; I have put my hope in your word."* God's promises restore hope and remind you of His faithfulness, even when life feels overwhelming.

### 4. **The Word Guards Your Mind**

Philippians 4:8 urges believers to focus on what is true, noble, right, pure, lovely, admirable, excellent, and praiseworthy. Regularly meditating on Scripture helps you guard your mind against negative and destructive thoughts.

## Practical Steps to Renew Your Mind

### 1. **Identify Negative Thought Patterns**

Take time to recognize recurring thoughts that are rooted in trauma, such as fear, self-doubt, or guilt. Write them down and compare them to God's Word.

Example: If you often think, *"I'll never be good enough,"* counter it with Ephesians 2:10, which says, *"For we are God's handiwork, created in Christ Jesus to do good works."*

### 2. **Memorize and Meditate on Scripture**

Choose specific Bible verses that address your struggles and commit them to memory. Repeat them throughout your day, especially when negative thoughts arise.

Example Verses:

- *"I can do all things through Christ who strengthens me"* *(Philippians 4:13).*

- *"God has not given us a spirit of fear, but of power and of love and of a sound mind"* *(2 Timothy 1:7).*

### 3. Replace Lies with Truth

Every time a negative thought surfaces, consciously replace it with a biblical truth. This process takes practice but becomes easier as you align your thinking with God's Word.

### 4. Speak God's Word Aloud

There is power in declaring God's Word over your life. Speak scriptures that affirm God's promises and your identity in Him.

### 5. Surround Yourself with Scripture

Place verses around your home, workplace, or anywhere you spend time. Seeing God's Word daily reinforces its truth in your mind.

### 6. Seek God in Prayer

Ask God to help you identify and overcome thought patterns that are not aligned with His truth. Pray for the Holy Spirit to renew your mind and guide you into all truth (John 16:13).

## The Role of Gratitude in Renewing Your Mind

Gratitude shifts your focus from what is wrong to what is good and true. Philippians 4:6-7 says, *"Do not be anxious about anything, but in every situation, by prayer and petition, with thanksgiving, present your requests to God. And the peace of God, which transcends all understanding, will guard your hearts and your minds in Christ Jesus."*

Keep a gratitude journal to record daily blessings and answered prayers. Over time, this practice will help rewire your brain to focus on God's goodness.

# Overcoming Obstacles to Renewing Your Mind

### 1. Discouragement

Renewing your mind is a process that takes time. When progress feels slow, remind yourself that God is faithful to complete the work He started in you (Philippians 1:6).

### 2. Spiritual Opposition

Satan often attacks your mind with lies and accusations. Ephesians 6:17 calls the Word of God the "sword of the Spirit," equipping you to combat these attacks.

### 3. Lack of Consistency

It's easy to fall out of the habit of meditating on God's Word. Set aside daily time to read and reflect on Scripture, even if it's just a few minutes.

## Biblical Example: The Renewed Mind of Paul

The Apostle Paul faced tremendous suffering, yet his mind was anchored in God's truth. He wrote in 2 Corinthians 10:5, *"We demolish arguments and every pretension that sets itself up against the knowledge of God, and we take captive every thought to make it obedient to Christ."*

Paul's example shows that renewing your mind is an active, intentional process. Despite external circumstances, he chose to focus on God's truth and found peace in the midst of trials.

## A Prayer for Renewing Your Mind

*Heavenly Father, thank You for the gift of Your Word, which is alive and powerful. Help me to identify and overcome the lies that have taken root in my mind. Teach me to meditate on Your truth and replace negative thoughts with the promises of Scripture. Renew my mind daily and transform me into the person You created me to be. In Jesus' name, amen.*

## Key Takeaway: Renew Your Mind, Transform Your Life

Renewing your mind is an ongoing process that requires commitment and faith, but it is one of the most powerful tools for overcoming emotional trauma. As you immerse yourself in God's Word, you will begin to see yourself and your circumstances through His eyes.

With each renewed thought, you are taking a step closer to the freedom and peace that God desires for you. Let the truth of His Word be the foundation of your healing, guiding you toward a life filled with hope, joy, and purpose.

# Chapter 8:

# The Power of Prayer and Worship

Prayer and worship are transformative practices that connect us to the heart of God and invite His healing presence into our lives. For those dealing with emotional trauma, these spiritual disciplines serve as both a refuge and a weapon. They create space for God's peace, shift our focus from pain to His promises, and usher in freedom and joy. This chapter explores how prayer and worship become powerful tools for overcoming trauma and embracing God's healing.

## Prayer: Communing with God

### 1. Pouring Out Your Heart

Prayer is an intimate conversation with God. It's a space where you can be fully transparent, bringing your pain, fears, and questions before Him. Psalm 62:8 reminds us, *"Trust in him at all times, you people; pour out your hearts to him, for God is our refuge."*

When you pray, you acknowledge your dependence on God. Prayer provides a release for your emotions, allowing you to express your grief, anger, or confusion to a loving Father who cares deeply for you. In your honesty, God meets you with comfort and assurance.

### 2. Casting Your Burdens on Him

Emotional trauma often leaves us carrying heavy burdens, but prayer offers us a way to hand those burdens over to God. 1

Peter 5:7 encourages us, *"Cast all your anxiety on him because he cares for you."*

Through prayer, you surrender what you cannot control, trusting God to provide strength and solutions. As you release your burdens, you'll find that He replaces your anxiety with His peace and perspective.

3. **The Power of Intercession**

When you feel too broken to pray for yourself, others can intercede on your behalf. Similarly, praying for others not only brings their needs before God but also shifts your focus outward, reminding you that you are not alone in your struggles. Prayer strengthens bonds, builds faith, and invites God to work powerfully in every situation.

## Worship: Shifting the Atmosphere

1. **Worship as a Weapon**

Worship is more than singing songs; it is a declaration of God's sovereignty and goodness in the face of your pain. When you worship, you align your heart with God's truth, declaring His power over your circumstances.

Jehoshaphat's story in 2 Chronicles 20 shows the power of worship in times of battle. Facing a vast enemy, the king appointed singers to lead the army in worship. As they praised God, He fought their battle for them. Similarly, your worship invites God to work in your life, bringing victory over trauma and despair.

## 2. Finding Joy in God's Presence

Worship ushers you into the presence of God, where healing and joy abound. Psalm 16:11 proclaims, *"You make known to me the path of life; you will fill me with joy in your presence, with eternal pleasures at your right hand."*

Even in the midst of pain, worship reminds you of the joy that comes from being in relationship with God. It shifts your focus from what is wrong to the One who makes all things right.

## 3. Freedom Through Praise

Worship breaks chains of bondage. Acts 16:25-26 tells the story of Paul and Silas, who worshipped God while imprisoned. As they sang, the prison doors flew open, and their chains fell off. Worship has the same power in your life. When you lift your voice in praise, the spiritual chains of fear, hopelessness, and despair begin to fall away.

# Practical Steps to Cultivate Prayer and Worship

## 1. Establish a Daily Prayer Routine

Set aside time each day to meet with God in prayer. Whether in the morning, evening, or throughout the day, consistency is key. Begin with gratitude, present your requests, and take time to listen for His voice.

## 2. Create a Worship Playlist

Music has a unique way of lifting your spirit. Create a playlist of worship songs that resonate with your heart and remind you of God's faithfulness. Let the lyrics guide your thoughts and draw you closer to Him.

3. **Combine Prayer and Worship**

Prayer and worship go hand in hand. As you sing songs of praise, pause to pray the lyrics over your life. For example, if a song declares, *"You are my healer,"* turn it into a prayer: *"Lord, I trust You to heal my heart and restore my joy."*

4. **Worship in Community**

Attending church services, joining a small group, or worshiping with friends can strengthen your faith and remind you that you are part of a larger body of believers. Corporate worship magnifies God's presence and provides mutual encouragement.

## The Transformative Power of God's Presence

Both prayer and worship invite God's presence into your life, and His presence changes everything. In prayer, you hear His voice, feel His comfort, and gain His strength. In worship, you magnify His greatness, experience His joy, and witness His power.

Isaiah 61:3 speaks of God's ability to give *"a crown of beauty instead of ashes, the oil of joy instead of mourning, and a garment of praise instead of a spirit of despair."* Prayer and worship are the avenues through which God exchanges your pain for His peace, your despair for His joy, and your ashes for His beauty.

## A Lifestyle of Prayer and Worship

Healing comes not just from moments of prayer and worship but from making them a lifestyle. As you cultivate these practices daily, they become your natural response to life's challenges. Prayer keeps you rooted in God's love, and worship keeps your heart aligned with His purposes.

No matter where you are on your healing journey, prayer and worship are always available to you. They are the tools God has given to strengthen you, sustain you, and transform your heart. Lean into them, and you will discover the profound power of His presence to heal, restore, and renew.

## Closing Reflection

*Heavenly Father, thank You for the gift of prayer and worship. Thank You for hearing my cries and inhabiting my praises. Teach me to rely on these powerful tools, especially when I feel weak or overwhelmed. Help me to make prayer and worship a daily habit so that Your presence fills every part of my life. In Jesus' name, Amen.*

Let prayer and worship be your refuge, your weapon, and your pathway to healing. Through them, you will experience the power of God's love and the peace that surpasses all understanding.

# Chapter 9:

# Forgiveness and Freedom

Forgiveness is one of the most challenging yet liberating aspects of the healing journey. Emotional trauma often leaves us holding onto pain, anger, and resentment toward those who have hurt us—or even toward ourselves. Yet, forgiveness is not just about releasing others; it is about setting ourselves free. This chapter explores the transformative power of forgiveness and how embracing it leads to emotional freedom in Christ.

## Understanding Forgiveness

### 1. What Forgiveness Is—and Is Not

Forgiveness is often misunderstood, leading many to resist it. True forgiveness is not about excusing the wrongdoing, denying the pain, or forgetting what happened. It does not mean reconciling with someone who remains unrepentant or unsafe. Instead, forgiveness is:

- A decision to release someone from the debt of their offense.

- An act of obedience to God, rooted in His grace and mercy.

- A pathway to healing for your own heart.

By forgiving, you relinquish your right to seek revenge or hold onto bitterness. It is not about minimizing the harm done but about trusting God to be your justice and healer.

## 2. God's Call to Forgive

Forgiveness is not optional for believers; it is a command rooted in God's own example. Ephesians 4:32 says, *"Be kind and compassionate to one another, forgiving each other, just as in Christ God forgave you."*

When we remember how much God has forgiven us, it becomes possible to extend that forgiveness to others. This does not mean the process will be easy, but it does mean we have the power, through Christ, to forgive even the deepest wounds.

# The Cost of Unforgiveness

## 1. Bitterness and Bondage

Holding onto unforgiveness creates a prison of bitterness, anger, and resentment. Hebrews 12:15 warns, *"See to it that no one falls short of the grace of God and that no bitter root grows up to cause trouble and defile many."*

Bitterness corrodes your peace and joy, robbing you of the abundant life God desires for you. It keeps you emotionally tied to the person who hurt you, allowing their actions to continue to influence your life.

## 2. A Hindrance to Healing

Unforgiveness can also block your emotional and spiritual healing. Matthew 6:14-15 reminds us, *"For if you forgive other people when they sin against you, your heavenly Father will also forgive you. But if you do not forgive others their sins, your Father will not forgive your sins."*

This verse highlights how our willingness to forgive impacts our relationship with God. By forgiving, you open the door for His grace to flow freely into your life, bringing healing and restoration.

## Steps Toward Forgiveness

### 1. Acknowledge the Hurt

Forgiveness begins with honesty. Acknowledge the pain and the impact of the offense. Pretending it didn't hurt or suppressing your emotions will only delay the healing process. Bring your pain to God, trusting Him to walk with you through the journey.

### 2. Choose to Forgive

Forgiveness is not a feeling; it is a choice. You may not feel ready or willing, but through prayer and faith, you can choose to forgive. Philippians 4:13 assures us, *"I can do all this through him who gives me strength."*

Pray for God's help to release the person who hurt you. Say their name aloud in prayer, and declare your decision to forgive them. This act of faith invites God to work in your heart, even if your emotions have not yet caught up with your choice.

### 3. Pray for the Offender

Jesus commands us in Matthew 5:44, *"Love your enemies and pray for those who persecute you."* Praying for the person who hurt you may feel impossible, but it is a powerful step toward healing.

Ask God to bless them, to change their heart, and to bring them into His truth. Over time, these prayers will soften your own heart, freeing you from anger and resentment.

4. **Release the Outcome to God**

Forgiveness is about releasing the offender into God's hands. Romans 12:19 reminds us, *"Do not take revenge, my dear friends, but leave room for God's wrath, for it is written: 'It is mine to avenge; I will repay,' says the Lord."*

Trust God to deal with the person who hurt you. He is a just and loving God who sees every wrong and will make all things right in His perfect timing.

## Freedom Through Forgiveness

1. **Healing for Your Heart**

Forgiveness unlocks emotional and spiritual healing. It allows you to release the weight of the past and move forward in freedom. Psalm 147:3 declares, *"He heals the brokenhearted and binds up their wounds."*

When you forgive, you partner with God in the healing process. You create space for His peace and joy to replace the pain and bitterness that once occupied your heart.

2. **Restoration of Your Identity**

Unforgiveness can cause you to define yourself by your pain or the actions of others. Forgiveness restores your identity as a beloved child of God. It reminds you that your worth is not tied to what happened to you but to the unchanging love of your Heavenly Father.

3. **A Testimony of God's Grace**

When you forgive, you become a living testimony of God's grace and power. Others will see the freedom and joy in your life and be inspired to seek the same healing. Your story of forgiveness can point others to Christ, who makes all things new.

## Forgiving Yourself

Sometimes the hardest person to forgive is yourself. You may carry guilt, shame, or regret over past decisions or actions. But holding onto self-condemnation denies the power of Christ's sacrifice.

Romans 8:1 reminds us, *"Therefore, there is now no condemnation for those who are in Christ Jesus."* If God has forgiven you, you can forgive yourself. Release the weight of your past and embrace the freedom and new life He offers.

## Forgiveness in Action

Forgiveness is not a one-time event but a daily decision. Each time memories of the hurt resurface, choose to forgive again. Over time, the pain will lessen, and God's healing will take deeper root in your heart.

## Reflection Prayer

*Heavenly Father, I thank You for the gift of forgiveness. You have forgiven me of so much, and I am grateful for Your mercy. Help me to extend that same forgiveness to others, even when it is difficult. I release [name] into Your hands, trusting You to bring justice and healing. Heal my heart, Lord, and help me to walk in the freedom that comes from forgiveness. In Jesus' name, Amen.*

## Closing Thought

Forgiveness is not easy, but it is worth it. It is the pathway to freedom, healing, and peace. As you choose to forgive, you will experience the fullness of God's love and grace, and you will walk in the abundant life He has prepared for you.

# Chapter 10:

# Walking in Freedom Through the Power of the Holy Spirit

Healing from emotional trauma is not just about leaving the past behind; it's about walking forward in the freedom that God has designed for you. This freedom is made possible through the power of the Holy Spirit, who works within you to bring transformation, guidance, and strength.

In this chapter, we will explore how the Holy Spirit empowers you to live a life of freedom, how to cultivate a deeper relationship with Him, and how to rely on His power to overcome the lingering effects of trauma.

## What Does it Mean to Walk in Freedom?

1. **Freedom is Living Without Bondage**

Freedom doesn't mean you forget your past, but it means your past no longer defines or controls you. Galatians 5:1 declares, *"It is for freedom that Christ has set us free. Stand firm, then, and do not let yourselves be burdened again by a yoke of slavery."* Walking in freedom means refusing to be enslaved by fear, shame, or guilt.

2. **Freedom is Living in Purpose**

True freedom involves walking in the purpose God has for you. Trauma can cause you to feel stuck or directionless, but the

Holy Spirit leads you into a life filled with meaning and significance.

### 3.  Freedom is Living in Victory

Freedom does not mean the absence of struggles, but it means having the power to overcome them. Romans 8:37 reminds us, *"In all these things we are more than conquerors through him who loved us."*

## The Role of the Holy Spirit in Your Freedom

### 1.  The Holy Spirit as a Comforter

In John 14:16, Jesus promises, *"And I will ask the Father, and he will give you another advocate to help you and be with you forever—the Spirit of truth."* The Holy Spirit provides comfort during moments of pain and uncertainty, reminding you that you are never alone.

### 2.  The Holy Spirit as a Guide

The Holy Spirit leads you into truth and helps you discern God's will. John 16:13 says, *"But when he, the Spirit of truth, comes, he will guide you into all the truth."* When the path to healing feels unclear, the Holy Spirit offers direction and wisdom.

### 3.  The Holy Spirit as a Source of Strength

Trauma can leave you feeling powerless, but the Holy Spirit empowers you to face challenges with courage and faith. Acts 1:8 promises, *"But you will receive power when the Holy Spirit comes on you."*

### 4. The Holy Spirit as a Healer

Emotional wounds run deep, but the Holy Spirit works to heal and restore you from the inside out. Isaiah 61:1, a prophecy fulfilled by Jesus, states, *"The Spirit of the Sovereign Lord is on me... He has sent me to bind up the brokenhearted."*

## How to Cultivate a Relationship with the Holy Spirit

### 1. Invite the Holy Spirit Into Your Life

If you haven't already, pray and ask the Holy Spirit to fill your life. Ephesians 5:18 encourages us to *"be filled with the Spirit."*
*Prayer Example:*
*"Holy Spirit, I invite You into every area of my life. Fill me with Your presence, guide my steps, and help me walk in the freedom You provide."*

### 2. Spend Time in Prayer and Worship

The Holy Spirit responds to an open and worshipful heart. Spend time in prayer, praising God and asking the Holy Spirit to reveal His will and presence in your life.

### 3. Listen for His Voice

The Holy Spirit often speaks in a still, small voice or through the Word of God. Be attentive to His guidance, especially during times of prayer or Bible study.

### 4. Obey His Promptings

When the Holy Spirit prompts you to act, whether it's forgiving someone, stepping out in faith, or letting go of a harmful habit, obedience deepens your relationship with Him and reinforces your walk in freedom.

5. **Rely on His Power Daily**

Walking in freedom is not a one-time event; it's a daily choice. Galatians 5:25 says, *"Since we live by the Spirit, let us keep in step with the Spirit."* Lean on the Holy Spirit for strength and guidance every day.

## Practical Ways to Walk in Freedom

### 1. Let Go of Old Patterns

Breaking free from trauma involves letting go of thought patterns and behaviors that keep you bound. Ephesians 4:22-24 urges believers to *"put off your old self... and to put on the new self, created to be like God in true righteousness and holiness."*

### 2. Practice Forgiveness Daily

Even after making the choice to forgive, you may need to continually release lingering resentment. The Holy Spirit empowers you to forgive fully and walk in grace.

### 3. Speak Life Over Yourself

Proverbs 18:21 reminds us, *"The tongue has the power of life and death."* Speak words of truth and encouragement over your life, aligning your words with God's promises.

### 4. Stay Connected to God's Word

God's Word renews your mind and helps you stand firm against the lies of the enemy. Psalm 119:105 says, *"Your word is a lamp to my feet and a light for my path."*

5. **Surround Yourself with Supportive Community**

Healing is not meant to be a solo journey. Surround yourself with Spirit-filled believers who will encourage and support you as you walk in freedom.

## Overcoming Challenges to Walking in Freedom

1. **Fear of the Unknown**

Walking in freedom means stepping into a new way of living, which can feel intimidating. Trust in God's promise in Isaiah 41:10: *"So do not fear, for I am with you; do not be dismayed, for I am your God."*

2. **Relapses into Old Patterns**

Healing is a process, and setbacks may occur. When they do, lean on the Holy Spirit and remind yourself that God's grace is sufficient (2 Corinthians 12:9).

3. **Spiritual Opposition**

Satan will try to undermine your freedom with lies and discouragement. Ephesians 6:11 urges you to *"put on the full armor of God, so that you can take your stand against the devil's schemes."*

## Biblical Example: The Empowered Life of Peter

Peter's journey with Jesus was marked by failure and restoration. After denying Jesus three times, Peter felt broken and unworthy. But after receiving the Holy Spirit at Pentecost, Peter became bold and fearless, preaching the Gospel and leading the early church (Acts 2:1-41).

Peter's transformation shows the power of the Holy Spirit to take a person from a place of shame and fear to a life of freedom and purpose.

## A Prayer for Walking in Freedom

*Holy Spirit, thank You for Your presence in my life. Help me to walk in the freedom that Jesus has given me. Strengthen me when I feel weak, guide me when the path feels unclear, and fill me with Your peace and power. Teach me to trust You fully and to live in the victory You have promised. In Jesus' name, amen.*

## Key Takeaway: Freedom is a Journey Empowered by the Holy Spirit

Walking in freedom is not about striving in your own strength; it's about allowing the Holy Spirit to work within you. As you surrender to His guidance and rely on His power, you will experience healing, transformation, and the abundant life God has for you.

With the Holy Spirit as your Comforter, Guide, and Source of Strength, you can walk confidently into the future, leaving the chains of trauma behind and stepping into a life filled with hope, purpose, and joy.

# Chapter 11:

# Embracing Your New Identity in Christ

Healing from emotional trauma often requires more than releasing the pain of the past; it involves embracing the truth of who you are in Christ. Trauma has a way of distorting your identity, making you feel unworthy, unloved, or defined by your experiences. However, through Christ, you have been given a new identity—one rooted in His love, grace, and purpose. This chapter explores how to fully embrace your identity as a new creation in Christ and walk confidently in the freedom it brings.

## You Are Made New

1. **A New Creation**

When you come to Christ, you are not just forgiven—you are transformed. 2 Corinthians 5:17 declares, *"Therefore, if anyone is in Christ, the new creation has come: The old has gone, the new is here!"*

This truth is a cornerstone of your identity. You are no longer defined by your past, your pain, or what others have said about you. In Christ, you are made new, and your worth is found in Him alone.

2. **Freedom From the Past**

Embracing your new identity means leaving behind the labels and lies that trauma may have placed on you. Romans 8:1

reminds us, *"Therefore, there is now no condemnation for those who are in Christ Jesus."*

You are no longer condemned or chained to your past. God has set you free, and His truth overrides any narrative of shame, guilt, or fear.

## Your Identity in Christ

### 1. You Are Loved

At the core of your identity is this unshakable truth: you are deeply loved by God. Jeremiah 31:3 says, *"I have loved you with an everlasting love; I have drawn you with unfailing kindness."*

This love is not based on what you do or have been through; it is rooted in God's character and His choice to love you unconditionally. Embracing this love allows you to see yourself as God sees you—precious and valued.

### 2. You Are Chosen and Accepted

Ephesians 1:4-5 reveals that God chose you before the foundation of the world and adopted you into His family:
*"For he chose us in him before the creation of the world to be holy and blameless in his sight. In love he predestined us for adoption to sonship through Jesus Christ, in accordance with his pleasure and will."*

You are not an afterthought or a mistake. You are chosen, accepted, and cherished by your Heavenly Father.

### 3. You Are Empowered

As a new creation, you are empowered to live a victorious life. Philippians 4:13 reminds you, *"I can do all this through him who gives me strength."*

God equips you with His strength, wisdom, and Spirit to overcome challenges, walk in freedom, and fulfill His purpose for your life.

## Replacing Lies With Truth

### 1. Recognize the Lies

Emotional trauma often leaves us believing lies about ourselves. These may include:

- "I am not enough."

- "I will always be broken."

- "I am unlovable."

Identifying these lies is the first step to rejecting them. Write them down and bring them before God in prayer, asking Him to reveal His truth.

### 2. Speak God's Truth Over Your Life

Combat lies with the truth of God's Word. Scripture is a powerful tool for renewing your mind and solidifying your identity. Romans 12:2 encourages us, *"Do not conform to the pattern of this world, but be transformed by the renewing of your mind."*

For every lie you've believed, find a corresponding truth in Scripture. For example:

- Lie: "I am not enough."

  - Truth: *"I am fearfully and wonderfully made" (Psalm 139:14).*

- Lie: "I will always be broken."

  - Truth: *"He heals the brokenhearted and binds up their wounds" (Psalm 147:3).*

- Lie: "I am unlovable."

  - Truth: *"Nothing can separate me from the love of God" (Romans 8:38-39).*

3. **Declare Your Identity Daily**

Make it a habit to declare your new identity in Christ every day. Speak these truths over yourself in prayer, write them on sticky notes, or create affirmations based on Scripture. Let God's Word shape how you see yourself.

## Walking in Your New Identity

1. **Live in Confidence**

Knowing who you are in Christ gives you confidence to face life's challenges. You are no longer defined by your trauma but by the unshakable foundation of God's truth. 1 Peter 2:9 reminds you, *"But you are a chosen people, a royal priesthood, a holy nation, God's special possession, that you may declare the praises of him who called you out of darkness into his wonderful light."*

This confidence is not arrogance but a humble assurance of God's work in your life.

2. **Forgive Yourself and Others**

Embracing your new identity also means letting go of past mistakes—both yours and others'. God's grace covers all, and as you receive His forgiveness, you can extend it to others. This frees you from the chains of bitterness and regret, allowing you to live in the freedom Christ has purchased for you.

3. **Pursue God's Purpose**

Your new identity comes with a purpose. Ephesians 2:10 declares, *"For we are God's handiwork, created in Christ Jesus to do good works, which God prepared in advance for us to do."*

God has a plan for your life that is greater than your past. Embrace the opportunities He places before you and walk boldly into the future He has prepared.

## Reflection Prayer

*Heavenly Father, thank You for making me new in Christ. I release the lies of the enemy and the pain of my past. Help me to fully embrace my identity as Your beloved child. Teach me to walk in confidence, live in freedom, and fulfill the purpose You have for my life. I declare that I am loved, chosen, and empowered by You. In Jesus' name, Amen.*

## Closing Thought

Your identity in Christ is a gift that cannot be shaken by life's circumstances or defined by your past. Embrace the truth of who you are: a new creation, deeply loved, chosen, and empowered. As you walk in this identity, you will experience the fullness of God's love and freedom, becoming a light to others who need the same healing and hope.

# Chapter 12:

# Cultivating a Life of Joy and Peace

Healing from emotional trauma is a journey, but one of the most profound markers of restoration is the ability to live a life filled with joy and peace. These are not fleeting emotions tied to external circumstances; they are gifts of the Holy Spirit that flow from a heart deeply connected to God.

In this chapter, we will explore what it means to cultivate lasting joy and peace, how they serve as evidence of God's work in your life, and practical steps to sustain them even in the face of challenges.

## The Biblical Foundation for Joy and Peace

### 1. Joy as a Fruit of the Spirit

Galatians 5:22-23 lists joy and peace as fruits of the Spirit. These qualities are the natural result of walking with God and allowing the Holy Spirit to work in your life.

### 2. Peace that Surpasses Understanding

Philippians 4:7 promises, *"And the peace of God, which transcends all understanding, will guard your hearts and your minds in Christ Jesus."* This peace is not dependent on circumstances but is a supernatural assurance rooted in God's presence.

### 3. Joy in the Midst of Trials

James 1:2-3 encourages believers to *"consider it pure joy... whenever you face trials of many kinds, because you know that the testing of your faith produces perseverance."* Joy is not the absence of hardship but the presence of hope in God's promises.

## Why Joy and Peace Are Essential for Healing

### 1. They Reflect God's Character

Joy and peace are part of God's nature. When you experience them, you are aligning your life with who He is. Nehemiah 8:10 reminds us, *"The joy of the Lord is your strength."*

### 2. They Are Indicators of Freedom

When trauma no longer holds you captive, joy and peace naturally flow. They signify that you are living in the freedom Christ has given you.

### 3. They Are Powerful Witnesses

A life marked by joy and peace serves as a testimony of God's transformative power. Others will notice the difference and be drawn to the source of your hope.

## How to Cultivate Joy in Your Daily Life

### 1. Stay Rooted in God's Presence

Psalm 16:11 says, *"You make known to me the path of life; you will fill me with joy in your presence."* Spend time in prayer, worship, and meditating on God's Word to cultivate a sense of His presence.

### 2. Practice Gratitude

Gratitude shifts your focus from what you lack to what God has provided. 1 Thessalonians 5:18 encourages, *"Give thanks in all circumstances; for this is God's will for you in Christ Jesus."*

### 3. Celebrate Small Victories

Healing is a process, and every step forward is worth celebrating. Take time to acknowledge and rejoice in the progress you've made.

### 4. Engage in Activities that Bring Joy

God created you with unique passions and interests. Whether it's spending time in nature, creating art, or enjoying fellowship with loved ones, make time for activities that refresh your spirit.

### 5. Share Your Joy with Others

Joy multiplies when it's shared. Encourage others with your testimony and celebrate their victories as well.

## How to Sustain Peace in Challenging Times

### 1. Trust God's Sovereignty

Isaiah 26:3 promises, *"You will keep in perfect peace those whose minds are steadfast, because they trust in you."* Peace comes from trusting that God is in control, even when life feels uncertain.

### 2. Cast Your Cares on Him

1 Peter 5:7 says, *"Cast all your anxiety on him because he cares for you."* When worries arise, surrender them to God through prayer.

3. **Guard Your Heart and Mind**

Philippians 4:8 advises, *"Whatever is true, whatever is noble, whatever is right, whatever is pure, whatever is lovely, whatever is admirable—if anything is excellent or praiseworthy—think about such things."* Fill your mind with thoughts that align with God's truth.

4. **Establish Healthy Boundaries**

Peace often requires creating boundaries that protect your emotional and spiritual well-being. Learn to say no to situations or relationships that disrupt your peace.

5. **Be Guided by the Holy Spirit**

Romans 8:6 states, *"The mind governed by the Spirit is life and peace."* Allow the Holy Spirit to guide your decisions and responses to challenges.

## The Role of Worship in Cultivating Joy and Peace

Worship is a powerful way to connect with God and cultivate joy and peace. When you focus on God's greatness, your perspective shifts, and your heart is filled with His presence. Psalm 100:2 encourages, *"Worship the Lord with gladness; come before him with joyful songs."*

- **Sing Praises**: Even in difficult times, singing praises reminds your heart of God's goodness and faithfulness.

- **Reflect on His Promises**: Meditate on scriptures that affirm God's love, provision, and protection.

- **Surrender Through Worship**: Use worship as a time to surrender your fears and anxieties to God, trusting Him to provide peace in return.

## Overcoming Obstacles to Joy and Peace

### 1. Lingering Doubts or Fears

It's normal to struggle with doubt, especially after trauma. When doubts arise, remind yourself of God's faithfulness in the past and His promises for the future.

### 2. Negative Influences

Surrounding yourself with negativity can drain your joy and peace. Be intentional about the people and media you engage with, choosing sources that uplift and inspire you.

### 3. Unresolved Pain

Healing is not always linear, and unresolved pain can disrupt your peace. Bring these areas before God in prayer and seek wise counsel when needed.

## Biblical Example: Paul and Silas in Prison

In Acts 16:25, Paul and Silas were imprisoned for preaching the Gospel. Despite their dire circumstances, they prayed and sang hymns to God. Their joy and peace not only sustained them but also led to the miraculous opening of the prison doors and the salvation of the jailer and his family.

This story demonstrates that joy and peace are not dependent on circumstances but are rooted in a deep trust in God.

## A Prayer for Joy and Peace

*Heavenly Father, thank You for the gifts of joy and peace that come from knowing You. Teach me to cultivate these gifts in my daily life, regardless of my circumstances. Holy Spirit, fill my heart with Your presence, and help me to trust in Your goodness and sovereignty. Let my life be a reflection of Your joy and peace to those around me. In Jesus' name, amen.*

## Key Takeaway: A Life Anchored in Joy and Peace Reflects God's Healing Power

As you walk in freedom, joy and peace become the hallmarks of a restored life. They are not just emotional states but evidence of the Holy Spirit's transformative work within you.

By staying rooted in God's presence, trusting His promises, and cultivating gratitude, you can experience joy and peace that transcend life's challenges. These gifts empower you to live fully, reflect God's glory, and inspire hope in others.

# Chapter13:

# Community and Accountability

The journey of healing and growth is not meant to be traveled alone. God designed us for relationship, not only with Him but also with others. Community and accountability are vital components in overcoming emotional trauma and walking in freedom. They provide encouragement, perspective, and a support system as you navigate the challenges of healing. This chapter explores the importance of surrounding yourself with godly community and how accountability helps you stay on track in your walk with Christ.

## The Biblical Foundation for Community

### 1. God's Design for Connection

From the very beginning, God emphasized the importance of community. In Genesis 2:18, He declared, *"It is not good for the man to be alone."* While this verse speaks to the creation of marriage, it reflects a broader truth: we are not meant to live in isolation.

Ecclesiastes 4:9-10 underscores this:
*"Two are better than one, because they have a good return for their labor: If either of them falls down, one can help the other up. But pity anyone who falls and has no one to help them up."*

In times of emotional trauma, having others to walk alongside you provides strength, encouragement, and perspective.

2. **The Early Church Example**

The early church exemplified the power of community. Acts 2:42-47 describes believers gathering together, sharing their lives, and supporting one another:
*"They devoted themselves to the apostles' teaching and to fellowship, to the breaking of bread and to prayer."*

This model reminds us that healing and spiritual growth flourish in the context of shared lives and mutual support.

# The Role of Community in Healing

### 1. Encouragement and Strength

Healing from trauma can feel overwhelming, but being part of a supportive community reminds you that you are not alone. Hebrews 10:24-25 encourages believers to:
*"Consider how we may spur one another on toward love and good deeds, not giving up meeting together, as some are in the habit of doing, but encouraging one another."*

A godly community offers words of encouragement, a listening ear, and practical help when needed.

### 2. Perspective and Wisdom

Trauma can cloud your judgment and distort your thinking, but others can provide clarity and perspective. Proverbs 11:14 says, *"Where there is no guidance, a people falls, but in an abundance of counselors there is safety."*

Trusted friends and mentors can offer godly wisdom and help you discern the next steps in your healing journey.

3. **Prayer Support**

There is power in collective prayer. Matthew 18:20 reminds us, *"For where two or three gather in my name, there am I with them."*

When others pray for you and with you, it strengthens your faith and invites God's power into your situation.

# The Importance of Accountability

### 1. What Is Accountability?

Accountability is a commitment to transparency and mutual support in your walk with Christ. It involves inviting trusted individuals to speak into your life, challenge you when necessary, and hold you to the commitments you have made.

James 5:16 highlights the value of accountability:
*"Therefore confess your sins to each other and pray for each other so that you may be healed."*

While this verse focuses on confessing sin, it also reveals the healing power of vulnerability and mutual support.

### 2. Accountability Helps You Stay Focused

Healing is a process, and it's easy to get discouraged or distracted along the way. Accountability keeps you focused on your goals and encourages you to persevere, even when it's difficult. Proverbs 27:17 says, *"As iron sharpens iron, so one person sharpens another."*

### 3. Preventing Isolation

One of the enemy's strategies is to isolate you, making you feel as though you must face your struggles alone. Accountability combats this by ensuring you have people in your corner, reminding you of God's truth and your progress.

## Building Godly Community and Accountability

### 1. Finding the Right People

Not all relationships are equally beneficial. Look for individuals who:

- Share your faith and values.

- Exhibit spiritual maturity and wisdom.

- Are trustworthy and discreet.

- Genuinely care about your well-being.

These may include close friends, church members, mentors, or small group leaders.

### 2. Be Honest and Vulnerable

Healing and accountability require openness. Share your struggles, fears, and goals with your community. Vulnerability fosters trust and allows others to provide meaningful support. Galatians 6:2 encourages us to:
*"Carry each other's burdens, and in this way you will fulfill the law of Christ."*

### 3. Commit to Consistent Connection

Building community takes time and intentionality. Make it a priority to meet regularly with your accountability partners or small group. Whether through in-person gatherings, phone calls, or prayer circles, consistency strengthens your relationships and deepens trust.

4. **Pray Together**

Prayer is a powerful way to strengthen community and accountability. Pray for one another, asking God to guide, heal, and empower each person. Colossians 4:2 reminds us to:
*"Devote yourselves to prayer, being watchful and thankful."*

## When Community Feels Difficult

### 1. Overcoming Fear of Vulnerability

Opening up about trauma can feel intimidating, especially if you've been hurt in the past. Remember, God is with you in this process. Psalm 34:18 assures us, *"The Lord is close to the brokenhearted and saves those who are crushed in spirit."*

Ask God to guide you to the right people and to give you courage to share your heart.

### 2. Dealing With Disappointment

No community is perfect, and people may let you down at times. When this happens, seek God's guidance on how to address the issue and whether to continue the relationship. Ephesians 4:2-3 reminds us to:
*"Be completely humble and gentle; be patient, bearing with one another in love. Make every effort to keep the unity of the Spirit through the bond of peace."*

Extend grace, but also seek relationships that uplift and encourage you.

## Reflection Prayer

*Heavenly Father, thank You for creating me to live in community. I ask for Your guidance as I seek godly friendships and accountability. Help me to be vulnerable and honest with those You have placed in my life. Strengthen these relationships so they bring healing, encouragement, and wisdom. Teach me to support others as they walk their own journeys. In Jesus' name, Amen.*

## Closing Thought

Healing from emotional trauma is a journey best traveled with others. Godly community and accountability provide the support, encouragement, and wisdom you need to grow and thrive. As you open your heart to others, you will experience the beauty of shared burdens and the joy of walking together in Christ. Let community and accountability be the foundation for lasting transformation and freedom.

# Chapter 14:

# Living Out Your Purpose After Trauma

Healing from emotional trauma opens the door not only to personal restoration but to a deeper understanding of your God-given purpose. One of the most powerful aspects of overcoming trauma is the opportunity to step into the life God has uniquely designed for you, one that is marked by meaning, service, and fulfillment. This chapter will focus on how to discover, embrace, and live out your God-given purpose after trauma, using the gifts and strength God provides.

## Understanding Purpose in the Context of Trauma

### 1. God Has a Purpose for Every Season

Trauma can sometimes make you question your future or feel as though your past defines who you are. However, the Bible assures us in Jeremiah 29:11 that God has a plan for each of us, *"plans to prosper you and not to harm you, plans to give you a hope and a future."* Your purpose is not nullified by trauma but refined through it.

### 2. Purpose is Not Defined by Trauma

Your identity is in Christ, not in your pain. 2 Corinthians 5:17 declares, *"Therefore, if anyone is in Christ, the new creation has come: The old has gone, the new is here!"* Your past trauma does not define your future purpose; God does.

### 3.  God Redeems and Uses Pain for His Glory

One of the most profound aspects of healing is that God can use our pain for a greater purpose. Romans 8:28 reminds us, *"And we know that in all things God works for the good of those who love him, who have been called according to his purpose."* Your experiences, even the painful ones, can be used to help others find healing and hope.

## How to Discover Your Purpose

### 1.  Seek God Through Prayer and Reflection

God is the ultimate guide when it comes to discovering your purpose. James 1:5 encourages us, *"If any of you lacks wisdom, let him ask of God, who gives to all liberally and without reproach, and it will be given to him."* Through prayer and reflection, you can invite God to reveal His plan for your life.

### 2.  Understand Your Gifts and Talents

God has given you unique gifts and talents, and they are an important part of your purpose. 1 Peter 4:10 says, *"Each of you should use whatever gift you have received to serve others, as faithful stewards of God's grace in its various forms."* Take time to identify your strengths and passions, as these often point to the areas where God is calling you to serve.

### 3.  Look at Your Life Story and Experiences

Your past, including your trauma, can be a powerful tool for discovering your purpose. God often uses the experiences that have shaped us to guide us in serving others. For instance, if you have experienced grief, you may be uniquely equipped to minister to others who are mourning.

### 4. Seek Wise Counsel and Community

Sometimes, discovering your purpose requires the help of others. Proverbs 15:22 says, *"Plans fail for lack of counsel, but with many advisers, they succeed."* Seek out mentors, spiritual leaders, or trusted friends who can offer wisdom, encouragement, and perspective on how to live out your purpose.

## Overcoming Obstacles to Embracing Your Purpose

### 1. Fear of the Unknown

Stepping into your purpose after trauma can be intimidating. The fear of failure or the unknown may hold you back. But remember, God does not give you a spirit of fear, but of power, love, and a sound mind (2 Timothy 1:7). Trust that He will guide you, step by step, as you move forward in faith.

### 2. Feeling Unworthy or Inadequate

Trauma can leave you with feelings of inadequacy, but God equips and empowers those He calls. In Exodus 3:11-12, Moses questioned his own worthiness, but God reassured him that He would be with him. Similarly, God will equip you for the tasks He calls you to, no matter how unqualified or unworthy you may feel.

### 3. Lingering Shame or Guilt

Sometimes, shame from past experiences can block your sense of purpose. Yet, God promises in Romans 8:1, *"Therefore, there is now no condemnation for those who are in Christ Jesus."* Recognize that your worth and purpose are not dependent on past mistakes or traumas but on God's redeeming grace.

### 4. Discouragement and Delays

The process of healing and finding your purpose may not always be straightforward. You may encounter setbacks or delays, but this is part of the journey. Isaiah 40:31 promises, *"But those who hope in the Lord will renew their strength. They will soar on wings like eagles; they will run and not grow weary, they will walk and not be faint."*

## Steps to Living Out Your Purpose with Boldness

### 1. Embrace God's Timing

Your purpose will unfold in God's perfect timing. Ecclesiastes 3:1 says, *"There is a time for everything, and a season for every activity under the heavens."* Trust that He is orchestrating events in your life, and even in moments of waiting, He is preparing you for what's next.

### 2. Serve Others

Serving others is a powerful way to live out your purpose. Philippians 2:4 teaches, *"Let each of you look not only to his own interests, but also to the interests of others."* Whether through acts of kindness, volunteer work, or offering emotional support, serving others is central to fulfilling God's calling on your life.

### 3. Step Out in Faith

Purpose requires action. Hebrews 11:6 states, *"And without faith, it is impossible to please God, because anyone who comes to him must believe that he exists and that he rewards those who earnestly seek him."* Trust that God will lead you as you step out in faith, even when the path ahead seems unclear.

4. **Live with Intentionality**

Live each day with purpose, knowing that everything you do can bring glory to God. Colossians 3:17 reminds us, *"And whatever you do, whether in word or deed, do it all in the name of the Lord Jesus, giving thanks to God the Father through him."* Live intentionally, making each moment count toward fulfilling God's calling in your life.

5. **Trust God's Provision**

God will provide for the work He calls you to. Philippians 4:19 promises, *"And my God will meet all your needs according to the riches of his glory in Christ Jesus."* Trust that as you step into your purpose, God will equip you with everything you need to fulfill it.

## Biblical Example: Joseph's Journey to Purpose

The story of Joseph (Genesis 37-50) illustrates how God can redeem trauma and use it for a greater purpose. Joseph was betrayed, sold into slavery, and unjustly imprisoned, but God used those difficult circumstances to elevate him to a position of power where he could save countless lives, including the very brothers who betrayed him.

Joseph's story shows that trauma does not thwart God's plan; rather, God uses even the darkest moments for His glory and the fulfillment of His purposes.

## A Prayer for Purpose and Fulfillment

*Father, thank You for the unique purpose You have given me. I trust that You are using my experiences, both good and bad, to refine me for the work You have called me to do. Help me to embrace my calling with boldness and faith, knowing that You will equip me every step of the way. Guide me to serve others, reflect Your love, and live a life that brings glory to You. In Jesus' name, amen.*

## Key Takeaway: Purpose is Fulfilled in God's Timing and Strength

Living out your purpose after trauma may feel daunting, but with God's guidance and provision, it becomes not only possible but transformative. Your purpose is not defined by your past but is a gift from God that grows stronger as you lean into His strength and timing. As you serve others and live with intentionality, you will find deep fulfillment in the life God has prepared for you.

# Chapter 15:

# Walking in Wholeness

Wholeness is God's desire for every one of His children. It is the state of being complete and healed in every area of life—emotionally, spiritually, mentally, and physically. While emotional trauma may have left you broken and fragmented, God specializes in restoring what has been lost and making all things new. Walking in wholeness is not about achieving perfection but about living in alignment with God's design and purpose for your life.

This chapter explores what it means to walk in wholeness, how to maintain the healing God has started, and how to live in the freedom that Christ has already provided.

## Understanding Wholeness

1. **God's Promise of Restoration**

God's heart is for your complete restoration. Joel 2:25 declares: *"I will repay you for the years the locusts have eaten."*

This verse reflects God's power to redeem the broken places in your life. He does not just heal your wounds; He restores your joy, peace, and purpose, often making you stronger than before.

2. **Wholeness in Christ**

True wholeness is found in Christ alone. Colossians 2:9-10 reminds us:

*"For in Christ all the fullness of the Deity lives in bodily form, and in Christ you have been brought to fullness."*

When you accept Christ as your Savior, He fills the voids in your heart and brings completeness to your life. This wholeness is not dependent on your circumstances but is rooted in His unchanging nature.

## Maintaining Emotional and Spiritual Wholeness

### 1. Guard Your Heart

Proverbs 4:23 advises:
*"Above all else, guard your heart, for everything you do flows from it."*

Walking in wholeness requires being mindful of what you allow into your heart and mind. Protect your peace by:

- Surrounding yourself with positive, godly influences.

- Avoiding toxic relationships or environments.

- Regularly renewing your mind with God's Word.

### 2. Stay Anchored in God's Truth

Emotional trauma can leave behind lingering doubts or fears. Combat these with the truth of Scripture. Jesus said in John 8:32, *"Then you will know the truth, and the truth will set you free."*

Meditate on God's promises and remind yourself daily of your identity, worth, and purpose in Him.

### 3. Practice Gratitude

Gratitude shifts your focus from what is wrong to what is right. 1 Thessalonians 5:18 says:
*"Give thanks in all circumstances; for this is God's will for you in Christ Jesus."*

Keeping a gratitude journal or regularly reflecting on God's blessings can help you maintain a mindset of wholeness and contentment.

## Living in Freedom

### 1. Freedom From the Past

Walking in wholeness means no longer being defined by your past. Isaiah 43:18-19 encourages us:
*"Forget the former things; do not dwell on the past. See, I am doing a new thing!"*

God has already forgiven and redeemed you, so you can release the shame, guilt, or regret that may try to hold you back.

### 2. Breaking Strongholds

Freedom also involves breaking any lingering strongholds or habits that hinder your walk with Christ. 2 Corinthians 10:4-5 reminds us:
*"The weapons we fight with are not the weapons of the world. On the contrary, they have divine power to demolish strongholds."*

Through prayer, Scripture, and godly counsel, you can overcome any barriers to your freedom.

## Practical Steps to Walk in Wholeness

### 1. Daily Surrender

Walking in wholeness requires daily surrender to God's will. Luke 9:23 reminds us:
*"Whoever wants to be my disciple must deny themselves and take up their cross daily and follow me."*

Trust God to guide your steps and strengthen you as you follow Him.

### 2. Cultivate Healthy Habits

Wholeness involves caring for your entire being. Develop routines that nurture your physical, emotional, and spiritual health, such as:

- Spending time in prayer and worship.

- Engaging in regular physical activity.

- Maintaining a balanced diet and adequate rest.

- Seeking professional counseling or support if needed.

### 3. Stay Connected to Community

As discussed in the previous chapter, godly relationships are crucial for maintaining wholeness. Surround yourself with people who encourage you, hold you accountable, and point you toward Christ.

4. **Celebrate Small Victories**

Healing is a process, and progress often comes in small steps. Celebrate each milestone along the way and thank God for the work He is doing in your life.

## Reflection Prayer

*Heavenly Father, thank You for Your promise of wholeness and restoration. Help me to walk in the freedom You have provided and to align my life with Your design and purpose. Teach me to guard my heart, stay anchored in Your truth, and live in gratitude. Use my story for Your glory, and guide me as I pursue the plans You have for me. In Jesus' name, Amen.*

## Closing Thought

Walking in wholeness is a lifelong journey of growing closer to God and living in His freedom. It is not about being perfect but about being surrendered to His will and allowing His Spirit to work in you and through you. As you embrace His promises and walk in obedience, you will experience the fullness of life that Jesus promised—a life of peace, joy, and purpose. Let your wholeness reflect His glory and be a testament to His redemptive power.

# Chapter 16:

# Helping Others Heal - Sharing Your Story and Ministry of Restoration

One of the most powerful ways to live out your healing is by sharing it with others. As you experience restoration from emotional trauma, you become a living testimony of God's faithfulness, mercy, and transformative power. This chapter will explore the importance of sharing your story, the role of serving others in healing, and how you can use your experiences to minister to others in their own struggles.

## The Power of Your Testimony

### 1. Your Story is a Tool for God's Glory

Revelation 12:11 states, *"They triumphed over him by the blood of the Lamb and by the word of their testimony; they did not love their lives so much as to shrink from death."* Your testimony is a weapon against the enemy's lies. When you share how God has healed you, you declare that God is still working miracles today. Your story can encourage someone else who is walking through similar pain and remind them of the hope that exists in Christ.

### 2. Healing Through Vulnerability

Sharing your testimony requires vulnerability, but it is often in our vulnerability that true healing happens. 2 Corinthians 1:3-4 says, *"Praise be to the God and Father of our Lord Jesus Christ,* the Father of compassion and the God of all comfort, who comforts us in all our troubles, so that we can comfort those in any trouble with the comfort we ourselves receive from God." When you allow yourself to be vulnerable, you open the door for others to see God's work in your life and invite them into their own healing journey.

### 3. **God Uses Our Pain for His Purpose**

God does not waste pain. He uses it to shape us and to reach others. 2 Corinthians 4:7 reminds us, *"But we have this treasure in jars of clay to show that this all-surpassing power is from God and not from us."* Your brokenness and healing are part of a larger story that points to God's strength and glory.

## The Ministry of Restoration

### 1. **Calling Others to Healing**

God calls us to not only receive healing but also to help others walk in it. In Isaiah 61:1, the prophet declares, *"The Spirit of the Sovereign Lord is on me, because the Lord has anointed me to proclaim good news to the poor. He has sent me to bind up the brokenhearted, to proclaim freedom for the captives and release from darkness for the prisoners."* Jesus Himself was sent to bring healing to the brokenhearted, and He has now entrusted this ministry of reconciliation and restoration to His followers.

### 2. **Serving Others as an Act of Worship**

Serving others is not only an act of kindness but an act of worship. In Matthew 25:40, Jesus says, *"Truly I tell you, whatever you did for one of the least of these brothers and sisters of mine, you did for me."* Your service to others reflects your love for God and His work in your life. It is through serving that we become the hands and feet of Christ in a broken world.

### 3. Empathy and Compassion as Tools for Ministry

As someone who has walked through trauma, you are uniquely equipped to empathize with others in their pain. Hebrews 4:15 assures us that Jesus can empathize with our weaknesses. Because He understands our suffering, we can offer compassionate ministry to others who are hurting. Your ability to listen without judgment and offer a safe space for healing makes you a valuable instrument in God's hands.

## Practical Ways to Help Others Heal

### 1. Listen with Compassion

Often, the first step in helping someone heal is simply listening. James 1:19 reminds us, *"Everyone should be quick to listen, slow to speak and slow to become angry."* Many people simply need someone who will listen to their story without trying to fix it or offer advice. By being present and attentive, you validate their pain and offer the comfort of your care.

### 2. Offer Prayer and Spiritual Support

Prayer is a powerful tool for healing. James 5:16 encourages, *"Therefore confess your sins to each other and pray for each other so that you may be healed."* When someone is struggling, pray with them and for them. Sometimes, people may not have the words to pray themselves, but you can intercede on their behalf and ask God to bring healing to their brokenness.

3. **Provide Practical Support**

Healing goes beyond emotional and spiritual restoration—it often involves practical support as well. Galatians 6:2 says, *"Carry each other's burdens, and in this way you will fulfill the law of Christ."* This could mean helping with everyday tasks, offering resources for counseling, or providing meals for those who are struggling. Practical help shows love in action and can provide the space and time someone needs to heal emotionally.

4. **Encourage Forgiveness**

Unforgiveness can be a significant barrier to healing. Ephesians 4:32 calls us to *"be kind and compassionate to one another, forgiving each other, just as in Christ God forgave you."* As you help others heal, encourage them to forgive, not for the sake of the person who hurt them, but for their own emotional freedom. Forgiveness is a choice, and it's one that leads to restoration and peace.

5. **Guide Others Toward Professional Help**

Sometimes, the pain of trauma may require professional counseling or therapy. 1 Thessalonians 5:14 reminds us to *"encourage the timid, help the weak, be patient with everyone."* Encourage those struggling to seek help when needed, and don't hesitate to direct them to trusted Christian counselors or mental health professionals who can provide additional support.

## The Role of Community in Healing

### 1. Healing in Community

In Ecclesiastes 4:9-10, it says, *"Two are better than one... If either of them falls down, one can help the other up."* Healing is not a journey that should be walked alone. Being part of a church community or small group provides support, accountability, and encouragement. In these spaces, people can share their struggles, celebrate their victories, and grow together.

2. **Creating Safe Spaces for Vulnerability**

As a healer, you can help create safe spaces where others can share their stories without fear of judgment. Romans 12:15 instructs us, *"Rejoice with those who rejoice; mourn with those who mourn."* A community that is open and accepting provides the emotional support necessary for healing.

3. **Support Groups and Ministry**

Starting or participating in support groups is another way to minister to those who have experienced trauma. These groups allow individuals to share their stories, receive advice, and find healing in a group setting. Whether through prayer groups, Bible studies, or trauma recovery groups, these ministries offer a safe environment for people to walk through their healing journey together.

# Biblical Example: The Good Samaritan

In Luke 10:30-37, Jesus tells the parable of the Good Samaritan, where a man is beaten and left for dead, and a Samaritan stops to help him. The Samaritan doesn't just feel compassion; he takes action by providing care, shelter, and even financial help. This story demonstrates that our healing is not just for ourselves—it's to be shared with others. We are called to take action in loving and serving those who are hurting.

## A Prayer for Ministry to Others

*Lord, thank You for the healing You have brought into my life. Help me to use my experiences to help others find hope and healing in You. Give me a heart of compassion and a willingness to serve those who are struggling. Use my story for Your glory and let my life be a testimony of Your faithfulness. In Jesus' name, amen.*

## Key Takeaway: Your Healing Is a Tool for God's Kingdom

The healing you experience from trauma isn't just for your own benefit; it's an opportunity to help others find the same freedom and restoration. By sharing your testimony, serving others, and offering compassion, you actively participate in God's ministry of healing. Your story has the power to impact lives, draw others to Christ, and reflect the love and mercy of God in a broken world.

# Conclusion

## Embracing Healing and Purpose Through God

As we reach the end of this journey, remember that healing from emotional trauma is not a destination but an ongoing process, one that unfolds as you lean deeper into God's grace and embrace His plan for your life. Trauma can leave scars, but it also creates opportunities for growth, transformation, and restoration. The God who heals the brokenhearted and binds up wounds is the same God who will equip you for a life of purpose and meaning, even after trauma.

## Healing is a Process, Not a One-Time Event

It's important to remember that healing is not linear. There may be times when the pain feels as though it is resurfacing, but that does not mean you are back to square one. Healing is a continual journey of walking with God, renewing your mind, and choosing to believe in His promises despite your circumstances. Romans 12:2 encourages us, *"Do not conform to the pattern of this world, but be transformed by the renewing of your mind. Then you will be able to test and approve what God's will is—his good, pleasing, and perfect will."*

God's healing work in you is progressive, and as you continue to grow, you will see His faithfulness at every step. Your journey toward emotional wholeness may involve moments of challenge, but through each step, God is using these experiences to shape you into who He created you to be. Trust that He is making all things new (Revelation 21:5).

## Living in the Freedom of God's Love

One of the most profound gifts of healing is the freedom it brings. John 8:36 reminds us, *"So if the Son sets you free, you will be free indeed."* As you experience emotional healing, you begin to live in the freedom of God's love and His purpose for your life. This freedom allows you to move forward without the heavy burden of past trauma, fully embracing your identity in Christ.

Living in this freedom means not being bound by the shame, guilt, or anger of the past but instead walking confidently in the grace that God has extended to you. It means offering forgiveness, not just to others, but to yourself. And it means allowing God to use your story to impact the lives of others, knowing that you are no longer defined by your pain but by the hope and restoration you have found in Him.

## Your Purpose is Uniquely Yours

God has given each of us a unique purpose, one that is shaped by our experiences, our struggles, and our healing. Your journey through trauma has not disqualified you from God's call but has, in fact, equipped you to fulfill it with greater depth and understanding. Your purpose may look different from others, but it is no less significant. Ephesians 2:10 assures us, *"For we are God's handiwork, created in Christ Jesus to do good works, which God prepared in advance for us to do."*

You are an integral part of God's plan, and your life has meaning. As you continue to walk in healing, your purpose will unfold with clarity and boldness. Your story, your pain, and your healing are all part of the masterpiece that God is creating through your life.

## A Call to Minister to Others

Your healing is not just for you; it is a tool for ministry. God has called you to reach out to others, to comfort them with the same comfort He has given you, and to share the hope you have found in Him. As you help others heal, you will discover a deeper sense of fulfillment and connection to God's Kingdom. Through service, compassion, and the power of your testimony, you become a conduit for God's love and healing in the world.

2 Corinthians 1:4 reminds us that God comforts us *"so that we can comfort those in any trouble with the comfort we ourselves receive from God."* There is power in offering your story, in serving others, and in allowing God to use your life as a beacon of hope.

## Closing Prayer

*Heavenly Father, thank You for the healing work You have done in my life. Thank You for the grace, mercy, and strength You provide every day as I walk this journey. I trust that You are continuing to renew my mind and restore my soul. I pray for those who are still in the process of healing—that they would feel Your presence, Your comfort, and Your love. Help me to use my story and my healing to serve others and to bring glory to You. In Jesus' name, Amen.*

Healing is an ongoing process, one that brings us closer to God and helps us discover our purpose. The journey may not always be easy, but it is one that leads to freedom, peace, and the fulfillment of the life God has prepared for us. Keep trusting in God's faithfulness, keep walking in His grace, and remember that He is with you every step of the way. May you continue to live in the fullness of His love and share the light of His healing with the world around you.

www.ingramcontent.com/pod-product-compliance
Lightning Source LLC
Chambersburg PA
CBHW070759120626
46557CB00002B/670